23619

D0484287

THE JOURNEY TOWARD A VIRTUOUS LIFE

NOT THE END

But the

ROAD

GARY L. THOMAS

NAVPRESS®

BRINGING TRUTH TO LIFE

OUR GUARANTEE TO YOU

We believe so strongly in the message of our books that we are making this quality guarantee to you. If for any reason you are disappointed with the content of this book, return the title page to us with your name and address and we will refund to you the list price of the book. To help us serve you better, please briefly describe why you were disappointed. Mail your refund request to: NavPress, P.O. Box 35002, Colorado Springs, CO 80935.

The Navigators is an international Christian organization. Our mission is to reach, disciple, and equip people to know Christ and to make Him known through successive generations. We envision multitudes of diverse people in the United States and every other nation who have a passionate love for Christ, live a lifestyle of sharing Christ's love, and multiply spiritual laborers among those without Christ.

NavPress is the publishing ministry of The Navigators. NavPress publications help believers learn biblical truth and apply what they learn to their lives and ministries. Our mission is to stimulate spiritual formation among our readers.

ISBN 1-57683-603-7

Cover design by David Carlson Design
Cover image: Sivan Lewan/Photonica
Interior photos: Digital Vision
Creative Team: Greg Clouse, Darla Hightower, Pat Miller

Some of the anecdotal illustrations in this book are true to life and are included with the permission of the persons involved. All other illustrations are composites of real situations, and any resemblance to people living or dead is coincidental.

Unless otherwise identified, all Scripture quotations in this publication are taken from the HOLY BIBLE: NEW INTERNATIONAL VERSION® (NIV®). Copyright © 1973, 1978, 1984 by International Bible Society. Used by permission of Zondervan Publishing House. All rights reserved. Other versions used include: THE MESSAGE (MSG). Copyright © 1993, 1994, 1995, 1996, 2000, 2001, 2002. Used by permission of NavPress Publishing Group; the New King James Version (NKJV). Copyright © 1982 by Thomas Nelson, Inc. Used by permission. All rights reserved; and the Contemporary English Version (CEV) © 1995 by American Bible Society. Used by permission.

Thomas, Gary (Gary Lee)
  Not the end but the road : the journey toward a virtuous life / Gary Thomas.
    p. cm.
  Includes bibliographical references.
  ISBN 1-57683-603-7
  1. Virtues. I. Title.
  BV4630.T55 2004
  241'.4--dc22

                    2004002726

Printed in Canada

1 2 3 4 5 6 7 8 9 10 / 08 07 06 05 04

FOR A FREE CATALOG OF NAVPRESS BOOKS & BIBLE STUDIES,
CALL 1-800-366-7788 (USA) OR 1-416-499-4615 (CANADA)

Are you feeling depleted, like you're bored with Christianity? Or tired of

trying to measure up as a Christian? Wish you had a sense of Christ's

reality in your life? If that's your situation, learning how to grow in the

virtues of Christ can be a bridge to the new life you have wanted.

— GARY THOMAS

TABLE
OF
CONTENTS

Chapter One

ON THE PATH

※※※※※

*This life, therefore, is not righteousness, but
growth in righteousness, not health but healing, not
being but becoming, not rest but exercise. We are
not yet what we shall be, but we are growing
toward it; the process is not yet finished but it is
going on. This is not the end but it is the road; all
does not yet gleam in glory but all is being purified.*

— MARTIN LUTHER

CONVERSION IS JUST THE *BEGINNING* OF THE CHRISTIAN LIFE. THOUGH MOST OF US NAIVELY HOPED THAT TRANSFORMATION WOULD HAPPEN IN THE DAYS AND WEEKS IMMEDIATELY FOLLOWING

that step of faith, we quickly discovered that instant changes did not come, or they showed themselves briefly and then slid away.

The truth is, we need a *process* of renewal, a deep digging and infilling of our souls with something new so that on the site of our former life, a new life stands. We want God to take us — people who are stuck in old habits, trapped in the living death of boredom or irrelevance, possessed by our own possessions — and to deliver us from ourselves by a long miracle of spiritual transformation. We need Him to dig out those abrasive aspects of our character and replace them with a refreshing vitality, ultimately creating a new personality — the promised life of Christ in us.

Be encouraged. God is eager to be our "deliverer." He designed us to be His image bearers, each of us reflecting a particular aspect of Himself.

Pause for a moment and try to imagine yourself as a person who acts with the compassion of Christ; who has the patience of God Himself; who is discerning; gentle, yet confident; surrendered to the will and purpose of God. This is the life Jesus wants you to inherit, transforming you into a person who is motivated by the beautiful, not the lustful; the generous, not the selfish; the noble, not the conniving; the creative, not the destructive.

Is this the person you want to become? If so, there is an ancient and biblical practice by which the image and nature of God are restored in you.

PRACTICING THE VIRTUES

For centuries, Christian teachers have spoken about "practicing the virtues of Christ." By this, they mean imitating the inner orientations and behaviors evidenced in the life of Jesus while He walked on earth — toward the goal of a mature character. While salvation is a work that is done entirely within God's mercy and without human effort (see Romans 9:16), growth in Christ involves cooperation between God and His children (see 1 John 3:3; Philippians 2:12-13). Just as bodybuilders use weights to shape their physiques, so Christians can "work out" their faith by practicing the virtues, understanding that holiness won't "suddenly appear" just because they prayed a prayer of salvation.

The life Christ wants to grow in you is not founded on a list of do's and dont's, nor can it be accurately measured by yardsticks of spiritual performance — by how much you do or do not witness, or read your Bible, or attend church. (Indeed, if you approach the virtues as nothing more than obligations, you're going to labor without being able to rest.) And the life Christ wants to grow in you is most definitely not one of striving as you compare yourself to someone else. Despite your best intentions, unless you're carried along by God's power working within you, you'll be crushed by the seeming impossibility of spiritual growth.

The virtues are, quite literally, *God's* sculpting tools by which He slowly but surely shapes us into the image of His Son. To experience His life in us is to find our way into the life Jesus promised when He said, "I have come that [you] may have life, and have it to the full" (John 10:10).

How Does This Happen?

Of course, we can *know* the way to transformation but actually miss experiencing it on a personal level. We can live this entire life "saved" but relatively unchanged, starving our souls until they are limp and powerless.

Practicing and growing in the virtues of Christ and letting His nature feed us will ultimately create new habits of holiness. We press forward to grow in His attributes not out of fear, but because growing in His character is the path we travel to maintain intimacy with the Lover and Lord of our soul.

Taking off sin is an important component of Christian spiritual growth, but it's only the first step. After we "take off," we need to "put on." As the apostle Paul wrote, "You were taught, with regard to your former way of life, to put off your old self, which is being corrupted by its deceitful desires; to be made new in the attitude of your minds; and to put on the new self, created to be like God in true righteousness and holiness" (Ephesians 4:22-24).

Many of us know we cannot escape an old habit, or pattern of sin, by focusing on it and trying hard to avoid it. Before we know it, we've become sin-focused, and the energy we invest in trying to stop has the effect of a tire spinning in mud: Somehow we entrench ourselves deeper into the very act we're trying to stop. That's why any discussion of Christian growth apart from growth in the spiritual virtues is incomplete, maybe even detrimental. The virtues tell us what to put on — the attributes of Jesus. They sculpt the future and provide a much more healthy focus.

STARTING THE JOURNEY

The list of virtues chosen for this book has been based on the virtues recognized throughout the ages, though I make no claim that it is anywhere near exhaustive. Some well-known virtues (hope, for one) are not addressed. But the ones discussed here will certainly help you begin your exploration into the life-changing and spirit-transforming world of the virtues. So let's begin.

Father, I know I'm on my way to heaven, but I am still far too weighed down by the world. Help me to walk with you willingly on your pathway of growth, to delight in the process of holiness, and to experience the lightened load and maturity that the virtues bring to everyday living. Amen.

A [Christian] is shaped by virtues in the way that

others are shaped by pleasures.

—JOHN CLIMACUS

Clothing ourselves in Christ is the lifelong process by which

we put off the old and put on the new.

— GARY THOMAS

Continue to work out your salvation with fear and trembling, for it is

God who works in you to will and to act according to his good purpose.

— PHILIPPIANS 2:12-13

Chapter Two

THE VIRTUE OF HUMILITY

✦━━✦

The truth is this — pride must die in you, or noth-

ing of heaven can live in you.

—ANDREW MURRAY

Humble yourselves, therefore, under God's mighty

hand, that he may lift you up in due time.

—1 PETER 5:6

RELATIONALLY, THERE ARE FEW THINGS SO OBNOXIOUS AS SELF-RIGHTEOUSNESS. SPIRITUALLY, THERE ARE FEW THINGS SO INJURIOUS OR EVEN LETHAL AS PRIDE.

The irony is, the more we experience the character of Christ, the more natural reason we'll have to become prideful. If we're not careful, spiritual growth can sabotage itself. Perhaps that is why the great reformer John Calvin calls humility the "sovereign virtue . . . the mother and root of all virtue,"[1] and Jonathan Edwards, the renowned eighteenth-century American preacher, names humility the "most essential thing in true religion."[2]

If you've attempted to build a spiritual life from the outside in, bypassing humility, you probably feel tired, disillusioned, frustrated, or just plain lifeless. The solution isn't to neglect the outer disciplines (Bible reading, prayer, and so on), but to begin practicing the inner disciplines as well, beginning with Christ's foundational attitude of humility. Just remember: *We don't become humble as much as we learn to practice humility*. The virtues aren't a state of being. We enter into them by degrees, and perhaps nowhere is this as true as it is with humility.

RADICAL GOD-DEPENDENCE

From a spiritual perspective, humility is entering into the life of Christ from a radical God-dependence. It's an inner orientation of actively receiving from God and acknowledging our need. The humble Christian is the Christian who takes literally Christ's words: "Apart from me you can do nothing" (John 15:5). The nineteenth-century Scottish preacher Andrew Murray nails humility exactly when he calls it "the displacement of self with the enthronement of God."[3]

Humility is the disposition that makes us available to be blessed by God. The Psalms seem obsessed with God's eagerness to reach out to the humble: God saves the humble, guides the humble, sustains the humble, and even crowns the humble. Everything flows *from* God *to* the humble servant. Pride seeks to reverse this. Pride is self-reliance and self-dependence. Arrogance seeks to *obligate* God instead of *receive* from Him.

Many people, Christians included, have a distorted view of humility. Merely thinking ill of ourselves or making false, self-deprecating statements are not healthy spiritual exercises. As writer and theologian Peter Kreeft points out, "Humility is thinking less *about* yourself, not thinking less *of* yourself."[4] Being humble doesn't mean pretending we don't have gifts; Jesus never pretended that He was not the Son of God, yet He is the model for our own humility.

FORGETTING SELF

Humility goes beyond our vertical relationship with our heavenly Father to address our horizontal relationship with our neighbor. At the heart of "social humility" is self-forgetfulness. So often, we live as if the primary calling of the world and everyone around us is to make us happy, healthy, comfortable, and affluent. If anyone or anything dares to get in the way of this ultimate aim, we erupt into anger, resentment, and bitterness. Of course, the world doesn't revolve around any one of us, and the demand that it should do so creates nothing but frustration.

The inner discipline of humility acts like a filter, saving us from the tyranny of grossly unrealistic expectations that everyone and everything should bend our way. Self-forgetfulness also means we are liberated to serve others at God's direction, rather than trying to impress them. The ultimate picture of this is Jesus washing the feet of His disciples.

REMEMBERING GOD

The surest road to humility is a constant remembrance of God. When we don't take time to dwell on the power, beauty, holiness, awesomeness, and majesty of God, humility becomes a stranger, and pride becomes a raging force. Whatever it takes, create habits, rituals, and practices to intentionally remember God.

Next, practice humility toward others. Often, the smallest acts of a self-emptying nature perform the greatest work spiritually. Even trivial events — holding the door open for someone, letting a car slip in front of you during heavy traffic — can become the tests of eternity that help transform our hearts. Adopt the attitude of a servant, pray for those who inconvenience you, and meditate on the model of the apostle Paul: "Though I am free and belong to no man, I make myself a slave to everyone, to win as many as possible" (1 Corinthians 9:19).

The humble life is a life in which deep joy and profound appreciation — both for what God has given us and for what we in turn can give to others — become a daily occurrence because the wellspring of that joy isn't limited solely to our own personal happiness or good fortune. We can appreciate others without feeling diminished because they have skills we don't; we can revel in the beauty of a landscape without feeling envious that we don't own it; we can be fed by a well-preached sermon rather than fretting over the fact that we're not behind the pulpit. Selfless living is liberated living.

> *Father, Forgive me for my pride and cause me to put others' needs above my own. Help me to daily realize that the more I put my ego out of the way, the more your life, power, and purpose can pass through me. Amen.*

Unless we make the increase of humility our study, we may find that

we have been delighting in beautiful thoughts and feelings, in solemn

acts of consecration and faith, while the only sure mark of the

presence of God — the disappearance of self — was all the time wanting.

—ANDREW MURRAY

Arrogance can never be satisfied; you will never become God.

Humility can never be disappointed; if you want to serve someone,

you can always find someone to serve.

—GARY THOMAS

Chapter Three

THE VIRTUE OF SURRENDER

❧❧❧❧❧❧

Does obedience obligate God to bless us,

or can obedience call us to sacrifice? Think

about the Cross before you answer.

— GARY THOMAS

MANY OF US HOLD TO A "PRIMITIVE" CHRISTIANITY, IN WHICH EACH SIN MERITS A WHACK, AND EACH ACT OF OBEDIENCE MERITS ONE HEAVENLY BLESSING. WE THINK OBEDIENCE SHOULD LEAD TO

blessing after blessing until ultimately we become healthy, affluent, and happy.

But it's not that simple. Though Jesus promised many blessings, He also promised that there would be moments of sacrifice: "Everyone's going through a refining fire sooner or later" (Mark 9:49, MSG). When Jesus says *everyone*, He's excluding exceptions with a startling finality. He's saying there will come a time when you will be asked to sacrifice for your faith.

Sometimes we need to be reminded that our faith is based on the concept of sacrifice, beginning with Jesus. No one ever lived a more obedient life than Jesus, yet few have ever died such an inhumane death. Israel was enslaved for four hundred years — but never forsaken. The early Christian church was hunted, persecuted, and brutally beaten at various moments in its first century — but was always held with great affection by her God.

We don't choose the time or place in which we are born. Surrender to God's purposes is the interior attitude adjustment by which we can live above our time with an eternal perspective. People who live on the surface of life are ruled by circumstances, but surrender lifts us above momentary streams of events. As Paul said, "I have learned the secret of being content in any and every situation, whether well fed or hungry, whether living in plenty or in want" (Philippians 4:12).

Faith and surrender are based on the notion that God's good purpose will be worked out whether I see earthly blessing or not, and that in the meantime I can experience an interior peace that passes all understanding by adopting a childlike trust in Him.

Keeping Your Focus

One of the great difficulties of surrender is that God doesn't appear to treat His children equally. After Jesus' resurrection, He had a heart-to-heart talk with Peter and warned Peter about the kind of death he would face. Peter looked behind him and saw John, so he asked, "Lord, what about him?"

Jesus refused to answer Peter's question: "If I want him to remain alive until I return, what is that to you?" (John 21:19-22).

In this, Jesus tells you and me that we must surrender our jealousy and envy about God's plan for other people when those plans seem preferable to ours. It is when I compare my situation to that of others that I surrender the precious peace that God wants to give me.

Each of us will face different trials at different times, and these trials will cause us to change. Depending on our attitude, such challenges will leave us with an ugly, bitter, cynical, and mean spirit, or a stronger, more Christlike character. How we profit from or are crushed by our trials largely depends upon our state of surrender to God.

The virtue of surrender reveals the purity of our heart's motivation. If we come to God to be amply provided for, yet we find ourselves poor, we'll leave God. If we come to God to be made well, yet find ourselves sick, we'll leave Him. If, however, our motivation is simply to serve Him and glorify His name, no event in life can shake our faith, for God can be glorified in pain *or* pleasure, wealth *or* poverty, comfort *or* stress.

Seventeenth-century French mystic Jeanne Guyon realized that to experience a hard circumstance that goes against our will is a gift. When accepted with the right spirit, it becomes an important means to a higher end: the presence of God Himself. As Paul taught, we are coheirs with Christ "if indeed we share in his sufferings in order that we may also share in his glory" (Romans 8:17).

THE PROCESS AND POINT OF SURRENDER

The key to surrender is acceptance. At times, this acceptance will come only after bitter struggle. Don't despair. As Guyon writes, "Sometimes you may bear the cross in weakness; at other times you may bear the cross in strength. But whether you bear it in weakness or in strength, bear it!"[1]

Likewise, remember that we can just as easily practice surrender in the face of blessings as in the face of trials. Surrender means adopting the right inner attitude to *every* outer circumstance. "Whether it be weakness or strength, sweetness or bitterness, temptation, distraction, pain, weariness, uncertainty or blessing, all should be received as equal from the Lord's hand."[2]

Finally, surrender is not something we can achieve all at once. Don't discount the small battles, thinking you can win the war in one tremendous act of "giving it all up to God." Fifth-century Christian John Climacus warns, "To be unfaithful in the small things is to be unfaithful in the great."[3]

Father, I confess those times I resist your will, especially when it comes to traveling the paths of hardship and trial. Help me to learn to stop measuring my trials against my comforts, and instead measure my trials against their potential to draw me nearer to you and to make me more like Christ. Amen.

If you gave yourself to Him to be blessed and to be loved,

you cannot suddenly turn around and take back your life

at another season when you are being crucified! . . .

God gives us the cross, and then the cross gives us God.

—JEANNE GUYON

Any small act of surrender, spiritually speaking, may do more

good for you than a year's worth of external discipline.

—GARY THOMAS

Chapter Four

THE VIRTUE OF DETACHMENT

***

If you desire to undertake a devout life, you must not

only cease to sin, but also cleanse your heart from all

affections to sin. . . . Souls that are recovered from the

state of sin, and retain these affections . . . eat without

relish, sleep without rest, laugh without joy, and drag

themselves along rather than walk. They do good, but

with such a spiritual heaviness that it takes away

all the grace from their good exercises.

—FRANCIS DE SALES

IT IS ONE THING TO BE SURRENDERED. IT IS ANOTHER THING ENTIRELY TO BE *DETACHED*. SURRENDER IS AN ACT OF THE WILL, ACCEPTING PHYSICAL CIRCUMSTANCES OR SITUATIONS THAT GOD

has ordained and looking for His good purpose in them. Detachment means we stop finding our meaning and security in people, things, positions, money, and power so they no longer lure us into actions we know are unwise or unprofitable. It also includes the gradual shaping of our desires so that they are in line with God's will and instructions for what is spiritually healthy.

The most famous verse on detachment is probably Matthew 6:33: "But seek first his kingdom and his righteousness, and all these things will be given to you as well." Jesus is saying that the *focus* and *passionate attachments* of the believer will center on God's kingdom. Detachment is the attitude that helps us cooperate with God's work as He shapes our desires. Leaving our needs and wants in His hands, we come to rest in the knowledge that what is truly valuable to the soul can only be given by God Himself.

FREEDOM FROM WITHIN

Every day, out-of-order and out-of-control appetites hold us in their grip, some to a lesser extent, some greater. John of the Cross teaches that uncontrolled appetites wound us in two ways: They deprive us of experiencing and enjoying God's Spirit, and they "weary, torment, darken, defile and weaken"[1] us.

An undisciplined inner life — one that is attached to the world even as it seeks to fight it — is misery defined. We halfheartedly want to follow God and live holy lives, all the while surrounding ourselves with temptation. Sometimes, errant desires can become so strong that the desire itself becomes the issue. Once we finally do give in, we're surprised that the fulfillment wasn't nearly as sweet as the anticipation.

To be free from the power of sin, we need to look at the internal cause rather than just focus on the action. When a Christian falls today, 99 percent of the spiritual effort is spent trying to control the "stumbling" — that is, we focus on outer strategies to help us avoid the situations in which we sin. However, iron will — external discipline that creates physical distance but not spiritual deliverance — will meet with only limited success.

If you have been fighting sin unsuccessfully, in large part because while you offer up the action, you can't stop the craving, then you need the virtue of detachment. This virtue begins when we turn our eyes from the created to the Creator. Detachment means relinquishing every demand we place on things and other created beings. Demands are nothing more than spiritual chains, opening wide the door to frustration, disappointment, and even disillusionment. We must die to our demands and trust God to give us what we truly need. Whether God chooses to provide or to give us the strength to do without, we learn to rest in Him.

The Power of Detachment

How can we experience the virtue of detachment? It is an impossible task to slowly disengage ourselves from every errant passion. What we need instead is a powerful war of engagement, which we find by *attaching* ourselves to something else.

It's easier to leave something behind if you believe you've found something better. As humans, we don't exist very well in vacuums; we're sucked one way or the other by our passions, so — spiritually speaking — instead of seeking a passion*less* existence, we need to *more intensely focus* our affections. John of the Cross points out that the lure of the world can be so strong that "if the spiritual part of the soul is not fired with other more urgent longings for spiritual things,"[2] the soul won't be able (or it will simply lack the courage) to deny its appetites for the wrong things.

If you're not cultivating joy in God, you'll seek excitement in the world. If you're not experiencing the fulfillment of being a servant of all, you'll crave recognition and fame. If you're not hearing God's voice, you'll pine for false intimacy in ungodly relationships, whether through gossip or sexual immorality. Over time, through delighting in God and His kingdom, we train our souls to desire what is healthy, pure, and good.

Our Model, Jesus Christ

When we look at the model of Christian living — Christ Himself — we can immediately see how central detachment was to His existence.

Jesus detached Himself from heaven to become man. He detached Himself from His parents to take up the public ministry of the Messiah. He detached Himself from His people's favor to become their Savior. He detached Himself from spiritually experiencing His Father's presence so He could become sin for us. And He detached Himself from life on earth to die for our sins. Christ gave up so much, but gained even more, being exalted to the highest place and given a name that is above every name (see Philippians 2:9). Look for Him in the virtue of detachment.

As you may be starting to comprehend, the virtues of Christ do not stand alone; they build on each other. To truly experience the freedom of detachment, we must grow in the spiritual virtue of attachment — the virtue of love. We'll discuss that next.

> *Father, I never realized there is so much strength to be found in detachment — learning to let go not just of the action of sin, but of the desire that drives me. Increase my passion for you as I refuse to feed off the errant passions within me. It's only as I do this that I will truly be able to enjoy the physical world that you've created for our pleasure. Amen.*

He hates not the fruit, who delights in the root.

—JOHN OWEN

Instead of fighting a defensive war, go on the offensive. Replace your particular obsession with a healthy passion.

—GARY THOMAS

Delight yourself in the LORD, and he will give you the desires of your heart.

—PSALM 37:4

Chapter Five

THE VIRTUE OF LOVE

❦

The soul needs no other force to

draw it than the weight of love.

—JEANNE GUYON

[Love] never looks back, but keeps going to the end.

—I CORINTHIANS 13:7, MSG

WHEN IT COMES TO CHRISTIAN SPIRITUALITY, IDLING IN NEUTRAL IS A GRAVE DANGER. WE NEED SOMETHING THAT WILL OVERCOME THE LUXURIOUS ALLURE OF THE WORLD AND THE

many false gods that compete for our affections. What we need is the virtue known as *love*. Christian love means *focusing the energy of your soul on God*.

There's a wonderful example of this in Luke 7:36-50. A "sinful" woman, likely a prostitute, walked in on one of Jesus' visits with the Pharisees. Seeing Jesus, she fell before Him and astonished everyone by pouring out most of her life savings, spent on costly fragrant oil, over His feet. Obviously, she was not thinking about her financial future. She was enraptured, and the energy of her soul was centered on the Messiah. He had touched her in a way that no one else ever had or could, and she responded with beautiful and reckless adoration. That's love.

Becoming like Christ is a life's work. It requires the only energy in the universe that is inexhaustible: love, and in particular, the love of God. No less an intellectual than Jonathan Edwards warns, "Man's nature is very lazy, unless he is influenced by some affection such as love, hate, desire, hope or fear. These emotions are like springs that set us moving in all the affairs of life and its pursuit."[1] Without the engine of love, we will be lackadaisical about our faith and everything that matters.

ENEMIES OF LOVE

Many of us never choose to grow cold toward God; we just get caught up in everything else. We're overcommitted. Others of us keep love at arm's length because of apathy, anger and resentment, fear, or discomfort with emotions in general.

The "horror of horrors" in Scripture is a hard heart. In Mark 3:5 we read that Jesus was "grieved" over the Pharisees' "hardness of heart." We are told that, of all things, "do not harden your hearts" (Hebrews 3:8, NKJV). A hardened heart is one that has stopped feeling, one that is dead toward God, one that feels no passion — and so it evokes no obedience to His commands.

What will help us obey God's commands is an engaged heart, a heart that is enlarging in love, a heart that feels new things, and feels them more deeply than it did before. And an enlarged heart is exactly what God promises us in Psalm 119:32.

TO CHANGE A HUMAN HEART

We celebrate Paul's glorification of love in 1 Corinthians 13, but the man who wrote "the greatest of these is love" was just a few decades removed from passionately persecuting and murdering Christ's followers. We do damage to this passage if we give it a sentimental rendering or imagine Paul as a soft, somewhat effeminate man. Love is the force that powered the transformation of Paul's life.

Never underestimate the power of love to change a human heart. Such a radical reorientation results not from a change of mind, but from a change of passion and allegiance. In fact, our holiness never begins with rule keeping, but with a passionate relationship. If we love someone, we're reluctant to offend that person.

John Climacus urges us: "We should love the Lord as we do our friends. Many a time I have seen people bring grief to God, without being bothered about it, and I have seen these very same people resort to every device, plan, pressure, plea from themselves and their friends, and every gift, simply to restore an old relationship upset by some minor grievance."[2]

If we cultivate an attachment to God, our desire and thirst for temporal sins, bad habits, and sinful attitudes will slowly fade. Writes the seventeenth-century Puritan great John Owen, "The fresh taste of spiritual things keeps Christians from worldly contentments."[3]

We become attached and detached by degrees. As you go through your day, you can't consciously focus every minute on loving God. But you can keep a careful eye on the things you allow to draw your attention and your affections, the way you can responsibly monitor how many calories you consume or how much television you watch. Proverbs 4:23 says, "Above all else, guard your heart, for it is the wellspring of life."

Do you seek to develop a stronger attachment to God? If so, stop right now and pray, "Lord, give me a love for you that is more powerful than any hunger for sin." Do you think God will hear that prayer and say, "Let me consider whether I really want to answer that one"? Not a chance.

> *Father, Fire my heart with a passion for you that will never die out. May I be abhorred at the thought of offending you, and be eager to quickly return to you when I stray. You know the things that sometimes keep me from loving you. Move them out of the way, so that you — and you alone — fill my vision. Amen.*

Sin that believes in nothing, cares for nothing, seeks to know nothing,

interferes with nothing, enjoys nothing, hates nothing, finds

purpose in nothing, [and] lives for nothing . . . remains alive

because there is nothing for which it will die.

—DOROTHY SAYERS

Love has led individuals to abdicate thrones, relinquish inheritances,

and move to foreign lands. Attachment to another person is

a truly powerful experience, but attachment to God is

an experience that changes us forever.

—GARY THOMAS

Chapter Six

THE VIRTUE OF CHASTITY

❧

God is such a stickler about morality, not because

he wants to control our behavior, but because he

wants us to become the kind of people who can

see him and thus experience infinite joy.

—PETER KREEFT

In A world where lust has gone mainstream, chastity is the true alternative lifestyle. Preach perversion and people will die to defend your "rights." Preach chastity and

you'd better hire a lawyer. Sadly, lust is no more a stranger to the church than it is to our society.

To be *chaste* means, simply, to be sexually pure — whether married or single. As a heart attitude, it recognizes that because God created all of us, each person should be treated with respect and dignity. If lust leads some to abuse or demean people for their pleasure, then true chastity leads us to protect people for the sake of their wholeness. Sexuality experienced God's way leads to greater intimacy and wholeness; sexuality outside the bounds of marriage leads to alienation, pain, shame, and regret.

Battling the Beast

At the root of lust are a number of issues, among them idolatry (worshiping the creature instead of the Creator) and a hunger for power and control. But another factor is our desire for intimacy in a society that has grown disconnected, anonymous, and lonely. The temptation is to take shortcuts, and lust *looks* like intimacy — without all the necessary personal growth and responsibility. You don't have to worry about deep character issues such as forgiveness, humility, and patience. There's no need for a man to have to face his pride, disrespect, and selfishness when he looks at pornography. There's no need for a woman to face issues of pettiness and manipulation with the man who is starring in her latest romance novel. She'll never have to say, "I'm sorry I put you down in front of your friends."

So how can we face down this dark, driving force in our lives? Long ago, I found some very practical advice in the ancient writings of John Climacus, who said, "The man who struggles against this enemy by sweat and bodily hardships is like someone who has tied his adversary with a reed." But, "if he fights [lust] with humility, calmness, and thirst [for righteousness and God], it is as though he had killed the enemy and buried him."[1]

Peter Kreeft, a modern writer, understands this same dynamic: "Concentrating on gluttony does not usually cure gluttony, especially in its serious stages, for it focuses attention on the very addiction or obsession that we want to escape. The same principle is true for lust. Though it sounds irresponsible and simplistic, we must 'turn our back on our problem' and look to God as our joy, our end, our fulfillment, our all, for the simple reason that he *is*."[2]

If we focus on building a life of virtue — humility, detachment, love, generosity, patience, and the like — lust will lose its foothold in our hearts.

THE ROOTS OF CHASTITY

Just as lust has its roots, so does chastity.

First, recognize that as enchanting as bodily pleasure might be, such experiences will never fully satisfy, as our souls were created with a hunger and passion that will find their true fulfillment in God alone. Sex done God's way leads to thanksgiving and contentment; sex outside God's will separates us from what we most desire: Him. G. K. Chesterton once said, "The man who is knocking on the door of a brothel is looking for God." Until we understand our spiritual longings, we won't be able to responsibly manage our physical desires.

Second, freedom is found when we cultivate a taste for the long-term meaning God gives our lives, as opposed to the short-term excitements of the flesh. This doesn't happen overnight. If you've fallen in this area before, you are well aware of the turmoil, stress, and pain it brings. You're familiar with sin's tendency to over-promise and under-deliver. Armed with this knowledge, make a firm decision to forgo the sin "just this once." And try an experiment: Compare the twenty-four hours after making a holy choice with the twenty-four hours after the last time you gave in to lust.

Third, cultivate selflessness. Lust is a self-centered sin, and it is not overcome by a self-centered repentance. The solution is to consider others, asking God to give you a respectful *reverence* for the people He has made. Remember: That man or woman you are abusing, either in practice or in your thoughts, is someone He is passionate about and whom He loves very much. Think of their well-being instead of your own satisfaction.

Finally, practice healthy sexual expression. Chastity is too often associated with a prudish attitude that sex is dirty and distasteful, yet the Bible celebrates marital sexuality by devoting an entire book to the subject (Song of Songs). Take all the time, energy, and money you spend on lust, and put it into a real relationship. If you're married, plan intimate times with your spouse. If you're single, use the energy and time to build real relationships based on selflessness, kindness, and purity, with a view toward one day fully enjoying the gift of marital sexual intimacy.

Chastity — in marriage or outside of it — is the channel that keeps sex pure, healthy, satisfying, and meaningful.

> *Father, The lusts of the flesh are ever before me. Help me to forsake these fleeting pleasures and their harmful consequences for a lifestyle of chastity. I want to be a person who is consistently building healthy, mature, and respectful relationships with you and the people you have placed in my life. Amen.*

Lust is our effort to push our way back into the garden.

— DAN ALLENDER

Flee from sexual immorality. All other sins a man commits are outside

his body, but he who sins sexually sins against his own body. Do you

not know that your body is a temple of the Holy Spirit, who is in you,

whom you have received from God? You are not your own; you were

bought at a price. Therefore honor God with your body.

— I CORINTHIANS 6:18-20

Chapter Seven

THE VIRTUE OF GENEROSITY

❧

The man who thinks nothing of goods has freed

himself from quarrels and disputes. But the lover

of possessions will fight to the death for a needle.

—JOHN CLIMACUS

WE CANNOT LIVE WITHOUT POSSESSIONS. JUST TRY TO SURVIVE A TEXAS AUGUST OR AN ALASKAN JANUARY WITHOUT APPROPRIATE CLOTHES AND SHELTER. POSSESSIONS ARE NECESSARY, SO IT

is not sinful to desire certain things. Sin enters our hearts *not* when we begin desiring certain things, but when we desire them out of proportion to their true worth.

One of the dangers of greed is that it often doesn't set off the alarms that other sins do. Most people don't misinterpret sexual temptation; they know what they're facing. The lure of greed and materialism is more subtle. C. S. Lewis warns, "Prosperity knits a man to the world. He feels that he is 'finding his place in it,' while really it is finding its place in him."[1]

Does that mean it's wrong for Christians to aspire after better things? Not necessarily. If someone is locked in a dead-end job and if family needs really aren't being met, complacency is a precarious pulpit to preach from. On the other hand, what freedom is gained by transforming yourself from a "wage slave" into an emotional prisoner of a luxury car or the servant of a huge mortgage?

This is the fine line we walk: Maturity demands that every adult handle money and possessions, yet material things are just waiting for a shelf in our heart to open up so they can lay an illegitimate claim there. Where is freedom for the Christian? What is our protection? It's found in the Christlike attitude of generosity.

Do You Want Your Life Back?

Fulfillment comes in being vessels of the generous heart of God by giving of our wealth and substance. God didn't create the world as a "level" roulette wheel, where some get lucky and some don't, all by chance. The way He has created us and the way He has designed the nature of human fulfillment is such that "it is more blessed to give than to receive" (Acts 20:35). God made us this way. He says, "If you want your life back, *give it away.*"

It seems illogical, but it's true. Do you want your life back? Give it to God. Do you want contentment? Learn how to wisely give your money away.

To do this, we must let go of the false security and pride in ownership that possessions promise. We must regularly remind ourselves that money cannot buy our way into fulfillment; we're more likely to buy our way into boredom. Likewise, we must remember the temptations of wealth. The apostle Paul writes, "People who want to get rich fall into temptation and a trap and into many foolish and harmful desires that plunge men into ruin and destruction. For the love of money is a root of all kinds of evil. Some people, eager for money, have wandered from the faith and pierced themselves with many griefs" (1 Timothy 6:9-10).

Not only must we let go of what is false and fleeting, but we must hold on to what is true and lasting. *Learn to think eternally.* Grasping the reality of heaven is a great antidote to the soul-poison of materialism. *Experience the internal joy of giving.* This joy comes from taking on the attitude of Christ, who told us, "Freely you have received, freely give" (Matthew 10:8).

SPIRITUAL GENEROSITY

Material generosity is just the start of inner freedom. There is a spiritual generosity as well, a disposition that leads us to give and serve rather than crave to receive. The Spirit of Christ leads us into service and floods our hearts with the joy that comes from selfless giving.

It's humiliating to admit, but when I first started speaking and teaching in churches, I had "small man's disease" — I spoke because I needed to be validated. My sermon preparation was not substantially different, morally, from the vain primping some people go through so their looks can wow people in public.

The change in me came from a divine challenge. As I was praying for an event a number of years ago, I sensed God telling me just to love the people I'd be speaking to. It was a liberating weekend because I learned that there's a tremendous difference between a teacher who wants to impart something important because he cares for his audience and one who wants to make a great impression.

What about you? When you arrive at church on Sunday, are you there to give or to receive? When you show up for work, are you looking for others to notice you, or are you looking to notice others? When you arrive home from work, do you expect your family to circle the wagons around you, or do you pray, as one of my friends does, "Lord, give me the strength to be completely present with my wife and children"?

If your aim is to receive, you're going to be disappointed most of the time. We live in a world that is much too preoccupied with itself to pay others much attention. If your aim is to give, if you find your enjoyment in encouraging others, you will never want for fulfillment; there will always be plenty to give.

Father, Generosity is so counter-cultural in a world of getting and taking. I need your supernatural strength to daily balance "what I need" and "what I want." Make me more of a giver, remembering all you have given and continue to give to me. Amen.

When a creature is made into a god, it becomes a devil.

—PETER KREEFT

"Give, and it will be given to you. A good measure, pressed down,

shaken together and running over, will be poured into your lap."

—LUKE 6:38

Chapter Eight

THE VIRTUE OF VIGILANCE

❧

Watch your life and doctrine closely.

—1 TIMOTHY 4:16

When spiritual matters are involved, failing to

give due caution can be eternally fatal.

—GARY THOMAS

THE BIBLE CALLS US TO THOUGHTFUL LIVING IN WHICH WE PAY ATTENTION TO OUR SPIRITUAL HEALTH AND EXTERNAL RESPONSIBILITIES. OUR MONEY WON'T MANAGE ITSELF. RELATIONSHIPS

need to be cared for. Passion for God must be nurtured. Concern for the lost needs to be fed.

Traditionally, this careful attention has been called the virtue of *vigilance*. To be vigilant is to live with a mindfulness about life, our attitudes, and our actions. As Deuteronomy 4:9 teaches, "Only be careful, and watch yourselves closely so that you do not forget the things your eyes have seen or let them slip from your heart as long as you live."

Jesus Himself punctuated many of His teachings with a call to vigilance: "Watch out! Be on your guard against all kinds of greed" (Luke 12:15). "Watch out that you are not deceived" (Luke 21:8). "Watch and pray so that you will not fall into temptation" (Matthew 26:41).

We live in a complex and challenging world in which vigilance is essential. As the famous preacher J. C. Ryle warns, "This world is not a world in which we can do well without thinking, and least of all do well in the matter of our souls."[1]

BECOMING A FISHER OF THOUGHTS

Vigilance is the attitude that allows the Holy Spirit space and time to show us what's really going on inside us. "The vigilant [Christian] is a fisher of thoughts," John Climacus writes, "and in the quiet of the night he can easily observe and catch them."[2] So strong and rich in spirit are men and women who understand their own soul that Climacus describes the process of vigilance as "collecting wealth."

I like this last image because it removes vigilance from sounding so much like yet another obligation and presents it to us as the gift it is. That's because vigilance will sometimes show us we've sunken into a habitually bad mood or slipped into a terrible attitude. Sometimes we'll see how we've been actively courting temptation or have become overcommitted. Vigilance helps us assess the truth about our lives, so we can turn from our weaknesses and find divine help.

Indeed, the more serious we are about becoming mature Christians, the more spiritual warfare will intensify around us. Climacus explains it this way: "War against us is proof that we are making war. . . . When a man is just a private citizen, a sailor, a laborer on the land, the enemies of the King do not take up arms against him. But when they see him accept the King's seal, the shield, the dagger, the sword, the bow, the uniform of a soldier, then they gnash their teeth and do all they can to destroy him. So let us not be caught napping."[3]

It sounds almost antiquated to talk about the Devil's work today. In our "enlightened" culture we've moved beyond the work of Satan. Yet Jesus and His apostles provide frequent warnings about the fact that we have a spiritual enemy, and thus we are foolish if we neglect to watch out for his schemes.

The Christian classics provide equal testimony to the sin in our hearts. Puritan John Owen calls vigilance "a moral sensitivity to the weakness and corruption within us." He warns, "We need to recognize the evil of sin and the power of temptation to work against us. If we remain careless and cold, we shall never escape its entanglements. We need to constantly remind ourselves of the danger of the entry of temptation."[4]

Practicing Vigilance

Christian vigilance is not just about self-examination. You could read a business book or a psychologist's self-help book to learn how to do that. Christian vigilance involves a plea for divine revelation, for someone outside ourselves to show us the truth about what's going on in the sometimes murky depths of our soul. We cannot trust our own insight or lean on our own understanding — we need to acknowledge God.

Vigilance means ordering our outside world in such a way that we can nurture our inner world. It means we make spiritual health a significant factor in every decision. Ryle writes, "No place, no employment is good for you, which injures your soul. No friend, no companion deserves your confidence, who makes light of your soul's concerns." He adds, "Keep in view, morning, noon, and night, the interests of your soul. Rise up each day desiring that it may prosper; lie down each evening inquiring of yourself whether it has really made progress."[5]

I believe Ryle is suggesting that we use the natural rhythms of life (waking, eating, going to bed) to keep our souls in check. Vigilance is a subtle but definite state of mind, cultivated in many short times of prayer — moments in which we ask, "God, what's going on?" I call this "just checking in."

Finally, a word of caution: The attitude of vigilance is a tool to set us free in spirit so that we can love, enjoy, and serve God. It is not meant to make us neurotic, religious messes. We can live in the loving, transforming presence of God and learn how to become more aware of what's going on inside and around us *without* guilt, condemnation, or self-obsession.

Father, Help me to live honestly and courageously before you each day. Keep me always listening to what your Spirit reveals of my heart and motives. Amen.

It is not your diligence, it is not your examination of yourself that

will enlighten you concerning your sin. Instead, it is God who does all

the revealing. . . . If you try to be the one who does the examining,

there is a very good chance that you will deceive yourself.

—JEANNE GUYON

You may be careless about your soul; [the Devil] is not.

—J. C. RYLE

Chapter Nine

THE VIRTUE OF PATIENCE

❦

Impatience is an addiction to comfort, ease, and

our own will. Patience is the virtue God grants us

to help us live more realistically in a world

where many things go wrong and where

frustration is a common occurrence.

—GARY THOMAS

A MEDICAL STUDY PUBLISHED SEVERAL YEARS AGO DEMON-STRATED THAT MEN WITH INCREASED ANGER MORE THAN TRIPLED THEIR RISK OF HEART ATTACKS AND CORONARY DISEASE. DRS. REDFORD and Virginia Williams put it succinctly: "Anger kills. We're speaking here not about the anger that drives people to shoot, stab, or otherwise wreak havoc on their fellow humans. We mean instead the everyday sort of anger, annoyance, and irritation that courses through the minds and bodies of many perfectly normal people. [Under the wrong conditions] getting angry is like taking a small dose of some slow-acting poison . . . every day of your life."[1]

Two thousand years earlier, the apostle James warned of the unfulfilled desires and impatience that are the breeding ground for anger when he wrote, "What causes fights and quarrels among you? Don't they come from your desires that battle within you? You want something but don't get it" (James 4:1-2).

Impatience is an addiction to comfort, ease, and having our own needs met. If we're late driving to work or church, we want every other driver out of our way. If we have a headache, we want those around us to intuit this and speak softly. We even want the weather to fit itself around our planned recreation.

Anger is born when we store impatience over time. Being an at-home mom, with little kids who fight, cry, or demand things all day long, can irri-tate your desire for peace and order. Working for a corporation mired in mindless bureaucracy, where the wrong people get hired for the wrong jobs, can be enormously frustrating.

Life involves many conflicts. It is unrealistic, unhealthy, and spiritually suicidal to live life expecting everything to fall into place just for you. And life doesn't get out of the way simply because we become Christians. The sooner we accept this, the sooner we can begin to enjoy the benefits of patience.

SPIRITUALIZED IMPATIENCE

Patience also affects how we approach spiritual growth. Some of the more impatient among us want maturity *now*. One decision, one trip to the altar for a prayer and public commitment, and we want it over and done with. Vices out, virtues in!

What we fail to understand is that our hard-won struggles are the ones that go deep. By definition, struggle isn't easy. In fact, struggle often involves defeat — or at the very least, severe setbacks. But it's the process that reveals deeper truths about us, and working all the way through the process of change will bring a more glorious end.

While our natural tendency is to seek quick spiritual fixes, internally based change usually lasts much longer. What we need, ironically enough, is to be patient with ourselves as we learn patience. John Climacus writes, "I cannot say why it is that some people appear to be naturally inclined to [be mild-mannered]. Others have to fight hard against their own natures to acquire these, they have to force themselves on to the best of their ability, suffering occasional defeat on the way; and it seems to me that the very fact of having to struggle against their own natures somehow puts them into a higher category than the first kind."[2]

THE MECHANICS OF PATIENCE

The first step in learning to practice patience is accepting discomfort. The apostle Paul urges us to be "patient in affliction" (Romans 12:12). The growth of every virtue begins when we accept with humility what God allows to come our way. This does not mean merely putting a lid on our anger and resentment; it means crucifying our anger through the virtues of surrender and detachment. We must be ruthless with our complaining and stop entertaining immature, unrealistic expectations.

Second, we need to practice the discipline of forgiveness. Paul tells Timothy that Christ's patience is "unlimited" (1 Timothy 1:16). Think about that: *unlimited* patience. There's no breaking point with God. There's no "I've had it with you employees!" Why? God forgives us and lets us start over. Impatience erupts when we hang on to the past.

Third, we must build a pause into our reactions, giving ourselves time to do the all-important soul work of examining our motives and desires. The man who blows up when his wife's problem can't be solved right away may not want a relationship with a real human being. He just doesn't want to be bothered, forgetting that real relationships are full of bother! The woman who loses her temper because the waitress got her order wrong should seriously consider her heart attitude. Is she more concerned about being inconvenienced than she is over this busy waitress's emotional health? Hasn't she ever made a mistake herself?

Beneath all this lies the need for wisdom. Proverbs 19:11 tell us, "A man's wisdom gives him patience; it is to his glory to overlook an offense." This means that we can allow Christ's patience to shine through us when we better understand the nature of the world — that it is a place of disappointment and failure, a fallen existence in which things go wrong every day. By reminding ourselves of this fact, we become less surprised and therefore less annoyed when things go wrong.

Wisdom includes maintaining an eternal perspective. Impatience arises when we begin seeking all the ease of heaven here on earth. God will certainly reward us, but some of us must learn to wait patiently — even until heaven in some cases — to see it.

God is offering us a love relationship that won't shield us from trouble but will never leave us alone and powerless in that trouble. This is our inheritance as Christians. Yes, "patient endurance" is "ours in Jesus" (Revelation 1:9).

> *Father, I ask forgiveness for the many times I've been impatient with myself, others — and you. Create a holy space in my heart by growing the virtue of patience. Amen.*

Learn to suffer with patience. God will send frequent and

probably great suffering into your life. This is His doing;

He has chosen it; accept it.

—JEANNE GUYON

Learning to walk in fellowship with God, in the patient spirit

of Christ, will turn our irritable souls into sanctuaries of peace.

—GARY THOMAS

Be patient, bearing with one another in love.

—EPHESIANS 4:2

Chapter Ten

THE VIRTUE OF DISCERNMENT

❧❧❧

Hell itself is truth known too late.

—J. C. RYLE

Discernment covers our thoughts with the

presence, beauty, and fellowship of Jesus Christ.

We don't live an infatuated existence, but our

hearts are perpetually "warmed up," ready to enjoy

Jesus as He walks with us through the day.

—GARY THOMAS

THERE IS AMPLE EVIDENCE IN SCRIPTURE AND CHRISTIAN HIS-
TORY THAT HOLINESS AWAKENS EVERY FIBER OF OUR BEING, INCLUD-
ING THAT ELEMENT COMMONLY REFERRED TO AS *DISCERNMENT*. THE

presence of Christ gives us a clearer eye with which to see the truth about people and situations, providing rare insight.

Jonathan Edwards, the great New England preacher of the eighteenth century, writes, "The child of God is graciously affected because he sees and understands something more of divine things than he did before."[1] In this, Edwards merely echoes the psalmist: "You, through Your commandments, make me wiser than my enemies. . . . I have more understanding than all my teachers, for Your testimonies are my meditation. I understand more than the ancients, because I keep Your precepts" (Psalm 119:98-100, NKJV).

Spiritual understanding comes from adopting God's view of all things. God understands our motivations, our fears, and our longings. He also knows how the world is meant to work — the importance of relationships over possessions, commitment over excitement, the eternal over the tempo-ral. When we truly know God, listen to Him, and are conformed to His image, He reveals these insights to us.

John Climacus describes discernment as "a solid understanding of the will of God in all times, in all places, in all things; and it is found only among those who are pure in heart, in body, and in speech."[2] This understanding seeks to cultivate the intellect with the wisdom of God. It doesn't result in new doctrines or esoteric explanations of parables — God's wisdom doesn't change — but it *does* create an excellence of understanding and perception.

Jesus had this quality about Him. The Bible says people were amazed at Christ's teaching because He taught as one who had authority (see Matthew 7:29). His words shot into the human heart and revealed something people had never seen or heard before. We like to focus on the miracles Jesus performed, but even more fascinating to me is His fertile mind.

How can we grow in this quality of Jesus?

THE KEYS TO DISCERNMENT

Three of the keys to unlock the door to discernment are apprehending spiritual beauty, developing refined taste, and gaining experience.

God is not just beautiful — He is *beauty* itself. Just as men will do silly things to attract a beautiful woman, so we will do radical things to live in obedience to a beautiful God — if, that is, our eyes are opened to His beauty. Edwards says spiritual understanding begins with this sense of "spiritual beauty." "For whoever does not see the beauty of holiness cannot appreciate the graces of God's Spirit. Without this there is ignorance of the whole spiritual world."[3]

If someone cannot perceive light, he is blind. Light is a basic component of sight, so if you can't see it, you really can't see anything. In the same way, God's beauty is the basic component of spiritual understanding and insight.

If we miss that, we get used to, or even become enamored with, this fallen world. We'll value what we shouldn't value; we'll treat with contempt what is most precious. Our priorities will get out of whack and our understanding will be darkened accordingly.

Biblically, there is a connection between immorality and stupidity, lack of understanding, and denseness. When we don't revel in God's glory and acknowledge His superiority, greatness, and beauty, we spurn the standard by which every human action, thought, and deed must be measured. But if we are captivated by God, something that opposes God will begin to repel us, making holiness, quite literally, a matter of *taste*. Edwards explains, "If an unworthy or unholy action is suggested to the spiritually discerning, a sanctified eye sees no beauty in it nor is pleased with it. Sanctified taste will only be nauseated by it."[4]

Finally, as we *experience* the reality of Christ, the beauty of living by God's wisdom and ways, something transforming happens in us. We gradually stop becoming mere religious critics, faultfinders, and sin spotters. We become, instead, discerners of the hidden motives that bind men's hearts to sin and make their lives weak, mean, and miserable.

Do we want to present Christ to the world, or merely rules? Young people will not quit sexual activity outside of marriage simply because we make a compelling argument for how such an action assaults character. A married couple contemplating divorce will not likely respond to eloquent sermons on how the disintegration of marriage is ruining society. Such self-denial needs a full heart arrest to become effectual, so that their eyes can be opened to the true ugliness of their seemingly romantic actions. If we want a relevant ministry, we must be able to pass on experience.

SPIRITUAL MUSCLE

When we gain wisdom, our mind becomes an instrument of holy war, a spiritual muscle. Exercising my mind as a spiritual muscle, I remind myself *why* I need to respond in a holy manner. I think about my family, my reputation, my commitment to the Lord. I think about long-term spiritual fulfillment, building a life of meaning, and not offending the God who has shown me mercy.

Maintaining the mind of Christ is a choice that may involve considerable struggle. Sometimes, I have found that the mind of Christ is preserved only with a fierce determination: "I *will* set my mind on things above. I will *not* dwell on earthly things." Other times, it's a natural outpouring of God's current blessing.

But with the mind of Christ, I never go into spiritual warfare alone or defenseless. Jesus and the rest of Scripture agree: Use your mind as a muscle. Exercise it. Live thoughtfully. Become wise beyond your years by adopting the knowledge of Scripture and then forcefully calling it into play.

> *Father, Make me a vessel of your beautiful, freeing truths. Give me eyes to see, a heart to obey, and a mind that discerns all that you desire for my life. Amen.*

Do not conform any longer to the pattern of this world, but be

transformed by the renewing of your mind. Then you will

be able to test and approve what God's will is.

—ROMANS 12:2

Imagine what it would be like if, after someone met you, he was

influenced for the rest of his life. I can imagine nothing more

rewarding than to so experience the light of Christ that others

sense Him, even in the smallest way, in my living, in my

treatment of them, and in my words.

—GARY THOMAS

Chapter Eleven

THE VIRTUE OF THANKFULNESS

❧⸭❧

Grace always attendeth him that is truly thankful.

—THOMAS À KEMPIS

What fascinates me so much is that every time we decide to be grateful it will be easier to see new things to be grateful for. Gratitude begets gratitude, just as love begets love.

—HENRI NOUWEN

WILLIAM LAW, THE EIGHTEENTH-CENTURY ANGLICAN, ASKS AN INTRIGUING QUESTION: "WOULD YOU KNOW WHO IS THE GREATEST SAINT IN THE WORLD?" HIS ANSWER IS FASCINATING:

"It is not he who prays most or fasts most. It is not he who gives the most money . . . but it is he who is always thankful to God, who wills everything that God wills, and who receives everything as an instance of God's goodness and has a heart always ready to praise God for it."[1]

A Fuel That Powers the Christian Life

Thankful Christians have cultivated a view of God's goodness in which they believe that He can work through all things. In humility, they're willing to accept that their understanding doesn't define God's goodness, so even when things look bad, they find something to be thankful for.

This is right in line with Scripture. First Chronicles 16:8 urges us to "give thanks to the LORD." Ephesians 5:20 tells us, "Always give thanks to God the Father for everything, in the name of our Lord Jesus Christ." First Thessalonians 5:18 is even more direct: "Give thanks in all circumstances."

Thankfulness is one of the most beautiful and spiritually strengthening attitudes of Christ. It is true that God deserves our thankfulness, but duty and obligation are hardly good motivators. Thankfulness, as an attitude, is like a fuel that powers the Christian life and keeps us moving on the pathway of spiritual growth, even when the climb is steep and the trail rough. Unless we learn how to cultivate a thankful heart, we become stuck in bitterness. I like to think of thankfulness as God's "spiritual air freshener." It replaces the stale odor of resentment with clean, fresh-smelling air for the soul to breathe.

STEPS TO CULTIVATING A THANKFUL HEART

I've come to cherish the practice of looking for something to thank God for, but I confess it was no quick journey from being a constant complainer to becoming an active thanker. Several small but progressive steps led me onward. Each step was a little more difficult than the previous one, but each new one also produced an increased spiritual benefit.

First, *recognize the danger of not giving thanks.* The apostle Paul warned us of a people who knew God but who failed to develop the discipline of thankfulness. The results were disastrous. "For although they knew God, they neither glorified him as God nor gave thanks to him, but their thinking became futile and their foolish hearts were darkened" (Romans 1:21).

It's as dangerous for a Christian not to give thanks as it is for a driver to leave her seat belt disconnected. When accidents happen — and, eventually, they will — we'll be left unprotected. If we don't adopt thankfulness, we undermine our own spiritual stability by questioning whether God is, after all, a loving Father. The difficulty of our situation and even the frustration of relatively minor nuisances can cloud our spiritual vision and tempt us to reconsider spiritual absolutes that we know are true.

Second, *arm yourself with Bible verses that call us to give thanks*. The Word of God is what we need to renew our mind and to redirect it into a positive thought-flow. The verses quoted in this chapter, and many other verses, remind us of an important spiritual truth: While we cannot control our circumstances, we can control the lens through which we view them.

Third, *thank God for the easy things*. To begin seasoning my soul with thankfulness, I started with things that are easy to give thanks for: the beauty of the natural world, God's goodness in sending His Son to be my Savior, and the blessing of my family. When life feels flat, and I don't feel thankful, thanking God for the easy things helps me to redirect my focus. There comes a time when thinking about a problem loses its constructive nature and becomes fretting. When this happens, there is no better medicine for me than to take a break from my relatively small world and set my mind on higher things.

Fourth, *thank God for the way He used difficult things in the past to build you up in the faith and make you a stronger person*. If God allows us to traverse only flat spiritual ground, our spiritual muscles won't strengthen. Perhaps it's too difficult to thank God for a hard struggle while you are right in it, but you can look back and say, "God, you really helped me mature during that last difficult time. Thank you."

Fifth, *thank God for what He is doing through the hard things in your life today*. Soon enough, you will find you are able to thank God for what He is doing through the difficult circumstances in the present. Remember, there's a difference between thanking God *for* the difficult things and thanking God *in* the difficult things. As Romans 8:28-29 teaches, "And we know that in all things God works for the good of those who love him, who have been called according to his purpose. For those God foreknew he also predestined to be conformed to the likeness of his Son."

If we miss this, we miss everything. *It is God's will that we be conformed to the image of His Son.* Virtually any circumstance — however painful or pleasant — can be used by God to shape the character of Christ in us, and it is for that shaping that we can be thankful.

Finally, *practice giving thanks.* So much in this world pushes us to be disgruntled. I sometimes lag in the practice of thankfulness and have to remind myself that giving thanks is a discipline. As an act of my will, I must choose to dwell on good things, on the high qualities of my invisible but everpresent Father. I consciously bend my thoughts away from resentment and remind myself I must wait for God to work out His best plans for me.

Sometimes it helps me to pray prayers of thanksgiving out loud so I can hear the words of thankfulness. Once thankfulness becomes a habit, it takes on a life of its own and becomes a source of tremendous strength.

> *Father, When I begin wasting my time by worrying and complaining, remind me that you are at work no matter the situation. Fill me with a spirit of gratitude and praise. Thank you. Amen.*

Let the peace of Christ rule in your hearts. . . . And be thankful.

—Colossians 3:15

For many of us, thankfulness starts out sounding shallow and trite.

But the truth is, it leads us into a deeper journey with God than we

imagined, taking us down to the core reason why we are here: Is it

to fulfill our own purpose for living—or His?

—Gary Thomas

Chapter Twelve

THE VIRTUE OF GENTLENESS

❧❧❧

The Scripture speaks of no real Christian who has

an ugly, selfish, angry, and contentious spirit.

Nothing can be more contradictory than a morose,

hard, closed, and spiteful Christian.

—JONATHAN EDWARDS

As a parent showers tender care on a newborn infant, the apostle Paul commands us to demonstrate this same gentleness toward others. He says that as apostles — as

living examples of the character of Christ — "we were gentle among you, like a mother caring for her little children" (1 Thessalonians 2:7).

Gentleness is so crucial to the Christian experience that Jonathan Edwards suggests gentleness may well be called "the Christian spirit. It is the distinguishing disposition in the hearts of Christians to be identified as Christians. . . . All who are truly godly and are real Disciples of Christ have a gentle spirit in them."[1]

The Taskmaster vs. the Gentle God

Sadly, a harsh view of God leads us to often be brutal with ourselves and demanding with others. Many of us look upon God as sort of a celestial Mark Twain — brilliant, but not easy to work for. We see Him as ruthlessly demanding perfection and letting us have it whenever we fall short. We believe that anything less than perfection will be met with at least a good, sharp kick, or maybe even a serious disease, such as cancer.

The Bible tells us God is offended when we think of Him this way. Because God is the source of all virtue, we can't experience one of His qualities while denying that He personifies that virtue. To get on the path of gentleness, then, we need to understand the depths of our Lord's gentleness.

Indeed, when Jesus describes Himself in Matthew 11:28-30, gentleness tops the list: "I am gentle and humble in heart." One of the Old Testament prophecies concerning Him foretold that the Christ would not break a "bruised reed" or snuff out a "smoldering wick" (Isaiah 42:3). Even at its best, a reed is very weak, hollow, and fragile. A *bruised* reed depicts a spirit that is hanging on by a few threads. A smoldering wick depicts a spirit in which life and hope have all but vanished.

I've met many people like that, who feel as if one more shake will surely be their last and they'll fall apart. In businesses and churches, in stores and shopping malls, and even in ballparks, you'll see bruised reeds and smoldering wicks. Lonely, distant marriages; the ache of a child in rebellion; the seeming impossibility of ever making enough money to pay half the bills; the pervasive silence of God; the scars of past humiliation; two dozen people's worth of ailments in one body — the causes of bruised reeds are endless.

Do you ever feel as if you are "just making it?" If so, you may know the offensiveness of ungentle Christians who march onto the scene and make an already difficult situation intolerable. The guy who says, "Get over it." Or the person who glibly comments to a mother suffering a miscarriage: "Don't worry; Jesus took your baby to be with Him in heaven. You're young, you can have another." Or the legalist who charges, "Obviously, you wouldn't sin if you loved the Lord. Are you sure you're saved?"

These people come with verbal saws to remove spiritual slivers. That's not an accurate depiction of Jesus. Jesus is the One who can touch you without breaking you. Jesus can gently nurse you back to spiritual health: "I am gentle and humble in heart and you will find rest for your souls."

The Spirit of the God-Man, who was sent to reveal the nature of our Creator, was clothed with gentleness; and this virtue allowed Him to enter into the lives of broken, hurting people. He wants to give us this same capacity for compassion.

Becoming Gentle People

The Bible is clear that those who call Christ their master will display the virtue of gentleness. Philippians 4:5 tells us, "Let your gentleness be evident to all." Colossians 3:12 adds, "Clothe yourselves with . . . gentleness." Paul is even more direct in 1 Timothy 6:11, telling us to "pursue" gentleness.

Even the enemies of Christ, those who oppose Him and ridicule His followers, are to be treated with gentleness (see 1 Peter 3:15-16). Gentleness is not a bonus we give to the deserving; it is a debt we owe to all, even to fallen Christians. Paul counsels in Galatians 6:1, "If someone is caught in a sin, you who are spiritual should restore him gently."

Gentleness is much more powerful than the human failings of temper, anger, and hatred. Anger has a place in the Christian life, as does confrontation. But gentleness will have a far bigger role to play, for gentleness means understanding human frailty. It's a willingness to support, help, teach, and counsel with patience, until the other person becomes strong and mature. Gentleness also means the application of grace, and because grace is "unmerited favor," the true definition of gentleness is the application of unmerited favor.

Nobody, apart from God, is perfect. Your spouse will fail you. Your children will disappoint you. Your pastor won't meet your expectations. The time will come, therefore, when you have a legitimate gripe. You will be right, and they will be wrong. This is the crossroads of gentleness. Which path will you take? But before you make that decision, remind yourself of how God has treated you.

Father, Teach me anew the importance of a gentle spirit and how pleasing it is in your sight. May others see Christ in me as the compassion He demonstrated flows from my words and actions. Amen.

We can't shout people into righteousness.

—GARY THOMAS

The gospel isn't about winning an argument; it's about reconciling

people to God and to each other. Brutish force doesn't reconcile,

it divides; legalistic demands don't invite, they alienate.

Grace and gentleness build bridges.

—GARY THOMAS

Chapter Thirteen

THE VIRTUE OF FORTITUDE

❧❧❧❧❧❧

Cowards die many times before their deaths,

the valiant never taste of death but once.

—WILLIAM SHAKESPEARE

Fear overlooks God's active presence.

—GARY THOMAS

JUST AS COURAGE IS HIGHLY VALUED IN WAR, THERE IS A COMPARABLE SPIRITUAL VIRTUE THAT IS ESSENTIAL FOR LIVING THE CHRISTIAN FAITH, ONE THAT THE ANCIENTS KNEW AS

fortitude—inner strength and spiritual courage.

If you pick up a Bible concordance and look up the word *afraid*, you'll notice how often these three words appear in front of it: "Do not be. . . ." Virtually every time God calls someone to do something in Scripture, He pleads with him or her, "Do not be afraid." God tells Joshua to "be strong and of good courage; do not be afraid" (Joshua 1:9, NKJV). He tells Joseph, "Do not be afraid to take Mary home as your wife" (Matthew 1:20). He tells Paul, "Don't be afraid to keep on preaching" (Acts 18:9, CEV). In Jesus' teaching and conversation, it seems like He spends half His words telling people not to fear.

Why all this attention? Perhaps it's because cowardice is one of the great life-thieves of all time. Spiritual cowardice worms its way into our souls when our eyes become obsessively focused on our circumstances and we lose our interior vision of God as our soul's strength.

Whatever the cause of your fear—if you're overly timid, easily cowed, and afraid to speak up—you will find it extremely difficult, perhaps even impossible, to walk in the character of Christ. When I read about Jesus standing up among the Sanhedrin, boldly facing His enemies and courageously speaking the truth, I marvel at His fortitude. He knew the plots that were being hatched in their hearts. He knew these people would put Him to death. But He spoke truth all the same.

Likewise, glory shines in the Christian who refuses to give up. She's beaten, she falls, she stumbles, she cracks, she breaks, she bends, but through it all, she keeps getting up.

The Nature of Fortitude

Fortitude is more than forcing yourself to put on a brave face. A soldier making a seemingly courageous charge in battle could be acting out of sheer cowardice. Maybe he fears his fellow soldiers' taunts more than he fears bullets. He could be running *from* ridicule even more than he is running *toward* the enemy.

Christ's fortitude provides an internal power that gives us the strength to pursue a course that frightens the natural man inside us. For example, it is demonstrated by a dissatisfied wife who walks away from an affair that promises emotional satisfaction but spiritual devastation. Urgent longings in her heart tell her to abandon her vows, but, through fortitude, she has the courage to walk away from that affair and trust God to meet her needs — even though she knows she is returning to a distant marriage and an inattentive husband.

Fortitude gives us the strength to live in a world of cancer, disaster, atrocities, temptation, betrayal, and hardship, all the while maintaining a calm, steadfast spirit. One Christian might hear the words, "the tumor is malignant," and immediately his faith shatters and breaks. A Christian armed with fortitude will know that God can work even through this. Even though the immediate future seems bleak, he chooses to trust in the ultimate goodness of God.

Just as the virtue of discernment springs from meditating on the beauty of God, so the virtue of fortitude is born when we meditate on the greatness of God. From the psalms of Moses and David, we read about men making God the soul's fortress, shield, hiding place, dwelling place, high tower, and high rock. Because these men had made God their soul's *internal* fortress, they could take *external* risks. By meditating on the greatness of God, they feared losing their grip on God's presence more than they feared losing their physical lives. When we are lost in the greatness of God, we realize that there is no physical, emotional, or social loss so great that God cannot bring good out of it and compensate us in the next life.

A GOD-CENTERED ORIENTATION

For me, gaining fortitude was virtually synonymous with gaining a God-centered orientation. When I rely on my strength alone, I put myself at the center of the universe — *I* have to provide for my family, *I* have to make things happen in the church, *I* have to take care of myself. When I take on Christ's attitude of full trust in God, I learn to rest in His provision, purpose, and benevolence.

We need to learn to leave the outcome of our battles to the Lord. It is when we try to control outcomes that we fail to have real faith in Him. The fortitude of Christ gives us a supreme calmness, the ability to calculate in peace rather than frenzy, and the courage to take the steps we need to take to act as people of faith.

Father, How much better it is to rely on you than to trust myself to make everything turn out right. Help me to hear your still, small voice amid life's hard times and to remember you will willingly supply the courage and strength as I ask. Amen.

The LORD is my light and my salvation — whom shall I fear?

The LORD is the stronghold of my life — of whom shall I be afraid?

—PSALM 27:1

Few things will build intimacy with God as much as

facing your fears with Him.

—GARY THOMAS

Chapter Fourteen

THE VIRTUE OF OBEDIENCE

༺❀❀❀༻

Men question the truth of Christianity

because they hate the practice of it.

—ROBERT SOUTH

Sin, while promising to enlarge our experience,

actually ends up limiting it.

—GARY THOMAS

IF ONLY WE COULD PROVE THE SINCERITY OF OUR FAITH BY THE SPIRITUAL RAPTURES WE EXPERIENCE DURING WORSHIP, THE SUDDEN SPARKS OF INSIGHT THAT CLEARLY COME FROM GOD, OR

the depth of our feeling following conversion! But the shallowness of this is readily apparent. I can give my wife valentine, anniversary, and birthday cards like clockwork. I can say all the right words. But if I keep a mistress on the side, will anybody guess that I truly love my wife? Or will it matter at all that I wept with joy on our wedding day if, ten years later, I'm a chronically selfish and critical husband?

The great preacher Jonathan Edwards points us to the bare essentials: "The proper test of what a man really prefers is to see what he actually cleaves to and practices when given a choice. . . . [G]odliness consists not merely in having a heart intent on doing the will of God, *but having a heart that actually does it*. . . . It is absurd then to pretend to have a good heart while living a wicked life" (emphasis added).[1]

Or a halfhearted one.

When we face temptation and the core of our will is exposed, we must ask ourselves, *Do I love God, or not?* Jesus was refreshingly blunt: "If you love me, you will obey what I command" (John 14:15).

I tend to make excuses for my self-indulgence: "I was tired; I've been really stressed. If I had been in my right mind, and at full strength, I wouldn't have fallen." This kind of cover-up talk will not even get you by a good therapist, let alone God. The truth is not just that temptation hits us *when* we're weak, but it also assaults us *where* we're weak.

The best thing we can do for ourselves is to regularly strip away all our excuses and ask how we are doing in regard to obedience. Don't fool yourself. Don't play games. Be honest with yourself and with God. How are you doing, really, in terms of actual obedience?

SHRUNKEN LIVING

The draw to sin comes from the fact that we are spiritually hungry people who want to be, in Jesus' words, filled. Sin provides a temporary break from reality—a momentary hit that removes the pain of separation from God. But here's the tragedy: It ultimately pushes us farther from God, causing our spiritual emptiness to grow over the long run. God made us in such a way that *only* those who search after righteousness will be filled. We can't be filled by sin—but we often think we can.

If the primary pursuit of your heart is anything other than learning to cooperate with God in the outworking of your life, you will always lack fullness within and eventually will find yourself in desperate spiritual straits. The more you sin, the harder it becomes to stop sinning. If you stay away from that sin for a while, it will be easier to avoid it the next time. As J. C. Ryle points out, "There are two ways of going to hell; one is to walk into it with your eyes open—few people do that; the other is to go down by the steps of little sins — and that way, I fear, is only too common."[2]

If you want God to give you your life back, you must begin to pay attention to the "Do Not Enter" signs posted in front of certain behaviors, thought patterns, and attitudes. The virtue of obedience is your guardian and your protector to keep you from hurting yourself as well as others, not to mention to prevent you from offending your God.

Pleasing God

The path to obedience is a path that begins in the interior life — confronting our sin and submitting to God. Doing this gives us the power to embark on outer action: actually taking little steps of obedience. Let interior obedience begin building in your heart until it brings you to an external victory. One act of obedience builds momentum toward a fully virtuous life. John of the Cross explains, "An act of virtue produces in the soul mildness, peace, comfort, light, purity, and strength, just as an inordinate appetite brings about torment, fatigue, weariness, blindness, and weakness. Through the practice of one virtue all the virtues grow, and similarly, through an increase of one vice, all the vices and their effects grow."[3]

Remember, real obedience is cultivated and demonstrated over years and decades. Its genuineness is proven when obedience gets truly hard — your soul screams its defiance, but you pursue God nonetheless. Yet obedience is always life-giving. It strengthens us and renews our spirits in a quiet and steady way. Just try it and see!

Father, Forgive me for the times I have disobeyed you this week, this day.

Thank you that your mercies are new every morning, and teach me again

the freedom and joy that overflow when I choose obedience. Amen.

The Scripture plainly teaches that practice is the best evidence of the

sincerity of Christians. Our reason teaches us the same thing.

—JONATHAN EDWARDS

It's easier to align our actions with God's will when

our heart is set on pleasing Him.

—GARY THOMAS

Chapter Fifteen

THE VIRTUE OF PENITENCE

❧❧❧

You can rationalize sin; you can flirt with it, but

remember who you're flirting with. Sin is a date

from hell, and however much hell acts like

your friend, hell hates you with a passion

that is terrifying in its intensity.

—GARY THOMAS

JOHN THE Baptist and Jesus both came on the scene preaching the same message: "Repent, for the kingdom of heaven is near" (Matthew 3:2; 4:17).

The Christian's spiritual life doesn't begin with hope. It doesn't begin with chastity. It doesn't even begin with obedience. It begins, according to the book of Matthew, with penitence. Interestingly, the first two beatitudes in Jesus' famous Sermon on the Mount also are related to penitence. "Blessed are the poor in spirit, for theirs is the kingdom of heaven. Blessed are those who mourn, for they will be comforted" (Matthew 5:3-4).

Penitence is being willing to exchange my old view of the things that I think will give me inner life for the things from God that really will give life and health. It involves sorrow for going the wrong way and a willingness to turn toward the right way. It's a change of heart accompanied by a change of mind, perfected by a change of direction — all three changes bending toward the will of God.

Because penitence is the spiritual counterbalance that rights us after our failure to obey God, it is the virtue that keeps us connected to the life-giving fellowship of God. Penitence returns us to humble reliance as it releases in us a spirit of surrender.

But why is penitence so crucial?

A Dangerous Game

One of the reasons God views our turning from sin with such tender affection is that sin itself is so deadly. Sin pretends to be your friend, but it's a liar. Are you lonely? Sin has an answer. Frustrated? Sin has a delicious solution. Bored? Sin has a "cure."

And so we taste — just a little. We make friends with sin, never intending to sign up for a full-fledged membership. But what makes us think we can do business with evil and get away unburned? And sin is, after all, sin. Satan comes only to steal, kill, and destroy (see John 10:10). If we live in Satan's world, we'll be robbed, killed, and ruined.

The great value of penitence is that it keeps us out of the path of our soul's enemy, who wants to kill us. It directs us back into the path of God, in the obedient attitude of Jesus, who has come to give us life.

The Penitent Path

The first step toward penitence comes from wanting to experience the full design of God's life for us. It is not fueled solely by sorrow for our sins, but by the joy of *becoming*. God made us to become like Christ as we work to advance His kingdom on this earth. Any other end is a sad misuse of the eight or nine decades God gives us. This is the change of heart that makes up the basis of penitence — a desire to be properly aligned with God, to fulfill all His goals for us.

Second, we need to grieve over the lost years of our sin. We need to mourn the wasted hours, energy, and resources. This often involves simply taking the time to prayerfully and honestly examine what our sin has cost us and others — including how it offends God. Painful as it is, do not be afraid to let anguish wash over you. Eventually, it will wash through you and leave you ready to begin again.

The final step toward penitence is using God's design on our lives to inform our future choices. When we realize we were made to fly, we won't settle for less. Why give our bodies to sin when God has made them temples of His Holy Spirit?

THE BENEFITS OF PENITENCE

One of the chief benefits of penitence is that it becomes much harder, spiritually, to judge others or to hold a grudge. When we experience God's rich forgiveness, it becomes much easier to offer that forgiveness, even to the undeserving.

Another great benefit of penitence is an ironic one. Surprisingly, penitence is the spiritual prelude to true celebration. People caught up in the world are deadened by sin and are frequently numb to what is happening within them. Penitence sets us free to experience true contrition, but this is the gateway also to experience true joy.

Penitence also reminds us that we are God's children. It is the gateway to the virtue of humility, which we explained earlier as the chief Christian virtue. It is impossible to be proud and penitent. If you have difficulty experiencing the virtue of humility, go through the "back door" of penitence.

The last benefit of penitence may be the most important. I do not want to suggest that by "God giving us our lives back," the virtues point only to an earthly existence. In one sense, I've used this phrase figuratively, but in this sense, it once again becomes literal. Those who have never repented are doomed to eternal separation from God. Hell is real, an excruciating, disastrous, and eternal existence full of pain and futile longing. The thief on the cross had just one thing going for him, a penitent heart, and Jesus promised him that this was enough to enter paradise.

Finally, because the virtues are something we practice imperfectly rather than own, penitence serves as the crucial connecting link to keep us on the path of growth. We will fail, but God has provided for that with a precious virtue called penitence.

Father, Keep my heart ever eager to turn back to you. Please grant me real remorse when I sin; whatever comes my way, keep me on the path that leads to earthly peace and heavenly glory. Amen.

God, in hating our sin, is like a surgeon who hates the cancer only

because he loves the patient.

—PETER KREEFT

Turn to Me with all your heart, with fasting, with weeping, and with

mourning. So rend your heart, and not your garments; return to the

LORD *your God, for He is gracious and merciful, slow to anger, and of*

great kindness; and He relents from doing harm.

—JOEL 2:12-13, NKJV

NOTES

Chapter 2: THE VIRTUE OF HUMILITY

1. John Calvin, *Institutes of the Christian Religion* (Philadelphia: Westminster Press, 1960), II.2.11.
2. Jonathan Edwards, *Religious Affections* (Minneapolis: Bethany, 1996), p. 128. William Law urges us to make humility the constant, chief subject of your devotion. William Law, *A Serious Call to a Devout and Holy Life* (New York: Paulist Press), p. 278.
3. Andrew Murray, *Humility* (Springdale, Pa.: Whitaker House, 1982), p. 59.
4. Peter Kreeft, *Back to Virtue* (San Francisco: Ignatious Press, 1992), p. 100.

Chapter 3: THE VIRTUE OF SURRENDER

1. Jeanne Guyon, *Experiencing the Depths of Jesus Christ* (Auburn, Maine: The Seedsowers, 1975), p. 39.
2. Guyon, p. 43.
3. John Climacus, *The Ladder of Divine Ascent,* trans. by Colm Luibheid and Norman Russell (New York: Paulist Press, 1982), p. 106.

Chapter 4: THE VIRTUE OF DETACHMENT

1. John of the Cross, *John of the Cross: Selected Writings,* ed. by Kieran Kavanaugh (New York: Paulist Press, 1988), p. 72.
2. John of the Cross, p. 79.

Chapter 5: THE VIRTUE OF LOVE

1. Jonathan Edwards, *Religious Affections* (Minneapolis: Bethany, 1996), p. 9.
2. John Climacus, *The Ladder of Divine Ascent,* trans. by Colm Luibheid and Norman Russell (New York: Paulist Press, 1982), p. 77.
3. John Owen, *Sin and Temptation* (Minneapolis: Bethany House, 1996), p. 84.

Chapter 6: THE VIRTUE OF CHASTITY

1. John Climacus, *The Ladder of Divine Ascent,* trans. Colm Luibheid and Norman Russell (New York: Paulist Press, 1982), p. 172.
2. Peter Kreeft, *Back to Virtue* (San Francisco: Ignatious Press, 1992), p. 180.

Chapter 7: THE VIRTUE OF GENEROSITY

1. C. S. Lewis, *The Screwtape Letters* (New York: Macmillan, 1951), p. 143.

Chapter 8: THE VIRTUE OF VIGILANCE

  1. J. C. Ryle, *Thoughts for Young Men* (Amityville, N.Y.: Calvary Press, 1996),
     p. 33.
  2. John Climacus, *The Ladder of Divine Ascent,* trans. Colm Luibheid and
     Norman Russell (New York: Paulist Press, 1982), p. 196.
  3. Climacus, pp. 115, 117.
  4. John Owen, *Sin and Temptation* (Minneapolis: Bethany House, 1996),
     p. 122.
  5. Ryle, p. 48.

Chapter 9: THE VIRTUE OF PATIENCE

  1. Drs. Redford and Virginia Williams, *Anger Kills* (New York: Harper
     Perennial, 1994), p. xiii.
  2. John Climacus, *The Ladder of Divine Ascent,* trans. Colm Luibheid and
     Norman Russell (New York: Paulist Press, 1982), p. 234.

Chapter 10: THE VIRTUE OF DISCERNMENT

  1. Jonathan Edwards, *Religious Affections* (Minneapolis: Bethany, 1996), p. 105.
  2. John Climacus, *The Ladder of Divine Ascent,* trans. Colm Luibheid and
     Norman Russell (New York: Paulist Press, 1982), p. 229.
  3. Edwards, p. 109.
  4. Edwards, p. 113.

Chapter 11: THE VIRTUE OF THANKFULNESS

  1. Paul G. Stanwood, Austin Warren, William Law, ed. *William Law: A Serious
     Call to a Devout and Holy Life* (New York: Paulist Press, 1978), p. 218.

Chapter 12: THE VIRTUE OF GENTLENESS

  1. Jonathan Edwards, *Religious Affections* (Minneapolis: Bethany, 1996), p. 144.

Chapter 14: THE VIRTUE OF OBEDIENCE

  1. Jonathan Edwards, *Religious Affections* (Minneapolis: Bethany, 1996),
     pp. 179-180.
  2. J. C. Ryle, *Thoughts for Young Men* (Amityville, N.Y.: Calvary Press, 1996),
     p. 64.
  3. John of the Cross, *John of the Cross: Selected Writings,* ed. Kieran Kavanaugh
     (New York: Paulist Press, 1988), p. 75.

AUTHOR

GARY THOMAS (www.garythomas.com) writes and speaks internationally on the nature of the Christian life. A Gold Medallion winner and an adjunct faculty member at Western Seminary, his books have been translated into six languages. Gary lives with his family in Bellingham, Washington.